The Wealth Whisperer

The Wealth Whisperer

Petchinsky

The Wealth Whisperer: Unlocking Abundance with Everyday Actions

By: Matthew Petchinsky

Introduction: The Power of Perspective and Action

Abundance and scarcity are more than just buzzwords—they are mindsets that shape the way we view the world, approach opportunities, and make decisions. Understanding the differences between these two paradigms is crucial for unlocking your full potential and achieving the life you desire. Moreover, the small actions we take daily often hold the key to profound transformations, proving that monumental change does not require monumental effort. In this introduction, we will delve into the fundamental concepts of abundance versus scarcity and explore why even the smallest actions can create ripple effects that lead to big results.

Understanding Abundance vs. Scarcity

At its core, the abundance mindset is rooted in the belief that there are enough resources, opportunities, and successes to go around. It encourages collaboration, optimism, and resilience. This perspective allows you to see potential where others see obstacles, to focus on solutions rather than problems, and to embrace growth rather than fear limitations.

The scarcity mindset, on the other hand, is governed by fear and a sense of lack. It tells us that resources are finite, opportunities are fleeting, and success is a zero-sum game where someone else's win is our loss. This mentality fosters competition, hoarding, and self-doubt. Living with a scarcity mindset can limit your ability to take risks, build relationships, and trust in your own capacity to create abundance.

Imagine two individuals with similar circumstances but vastly different mindsets. The person with an abundance mindset sees setbacks as stepping stones, learns from failure, and finds creative ways to move forward. Conversely, the person with a scarcity mindset focuses on what they lack, magnifies their failures, and avoids taking risks for fear of losing even more. The outcomes of these perspectives are worlds apart.

Choosing abundance does not mean ignoring challenges or living in denial of reality. It means recognizing challenges while believing in your ability to overcome them. It means understanding that wealth, success, love, and fulfillment are not pie slices with only so many servings—they are boundless, ever-expanding opportunities that grow when nurtured.

Why Small Actions Create Big Results

When faced with large goals or significant challenges, it's easy to feel overwhelmed. We often mistakenly believe that achieving greatness requires extraordinary efforts or dramatic life changes. However, research and real-life success stories tell a different tale: small, consistent actions compound over time to produce remarkable results.

Consider the power of compounding interest in finances—a concept where money grows exponentially as earnings generate further earnings. The same principle applies to personal growth and achievements. Small daily actions, repeated consistently, accumulate into transformative changes.

Take, for example, someone who wants to improve their health. Rather than embarking on an extreme diet or intense workout regimen, they begin with small, manageable habits—drinking an extra glass of water each day, walking for 10 minutes, or swapping one unhealthy snack for a healthier option. Over weeks and months, these small changes build momentum, leading to significant improvements in their overall well-being.

Small actions are powerful because they are:

1. **Sustainable**: They fit seamlessly into daily life, reducing the likelihood of burnout or abandonment.
2. **Motivating**: Success from small wins creates a sense of achievement, reinforcing the desire to continue.
3. **Transformative**: Incremental changes may seem insignificant at first, but over time, they reshape habits, perspectives, and outcomes.

Even seemingly inconsequential decisions—choosing to read a book instead of scrolling through social media, reaching out to a potential mentor, or setting aside a few minutes for reflection—can create ripple effects that lead to unexpected opportunities and lasting growth.

By focusing on small, purposeful actions, you shift the narrative of your life. Each step you take toward your goals strengthens your confidence, builds resilience, and fosters an abundance mindset. You start to realize that the path to greatness is paved with small, deliberate choices rather than a single leap.

The Journey Ahead

As you embark on this journey of embracing abundance and harnessing the power of small actions, remember that transformation is a process, not an event. Each chapter ahead will guide you through practical strategies, real-world examples, and actionable steps to help you cultivate a mindset of abundance and create the life you envision.

Understanding the concepts of abundance versus scarcity and recognizing the potential of small actions are foundational to achieving your goals. Together, these principles will empower you to break free from limiting beliefs, navigate challenges with confidence, and unlock a future brimming with possibility.

Let this introduction serve as your compass—a reminder that the shift toward abundance begins within, and that greatness is not about grand gestures but about the courage to take the first step, no matter how small. The journey to abundance starts now.

Chapter 1: Your Money Story

Exploring Your Financial Mindset and Shifting from Scarcity to Abundance

Money is more than just currency; it's a reflection of your beliefs, values, and experiences. Your financial habits and decisions are shaped by your "money story"—a narrative that has been built over the years through cultural influences, childhood experiences, societal norms, and personal choices. To change your relationship with money and create financial abundance, it's essential to uncover and understand your money story, then actively shift your mindset from scarcity to abundance.

Exploring Your Financial Mindset

Your financial mindset is the lens through which you view, handle, and interact with money. It determines whether you see money as a tool for growth and freedom or as a source of stress and limitation. This mindset often operates subconsciously, yet it influences every financial decision you make.

What Shapes Your Money Story?

1. **Childhood Experiences**

   The way your family discussed—or didn't discuss—money likely plays a significant role in your financial beliefs. Were conversations about money open and educational, or were they secretive and filled with tension? Did you grow up hearing phrases like "money doesn't grow on trees" or "we can't afford that"? These early messages can foster a scarcity mindset, making you view money as a limited and elusive resource.

2. **Cultural and Societal Influences**

   Societal norms and cultural expectations often dictate how we perceive wealth and success. You may have been conditioned to associate wealth with greed or moral superiority, or you may have internalized messages about what is "deserved" based on factors like education, background, or luck.

3. **Personal Experiences**

   Financial triumphs and setbacks leave lasting impressions. A promotion that significantly increased your income or a period of debt and struggle may have solidified certain beliefs about what you're capable of achieving.

4. **Media and Peer Influence**

   Social media, movies, and advertisements often create unrealistic portrayals of wealth, leading to feelings of inadequacy or unfulfilled aspirations. Meanwhile, peers and colleagues may unintentionally influence your financial behaviors through comparison and competition.

Identifying Your Current Money Mindset

To begin rewriting your money story, you need to identify the beliefs that currently guide your financial behaviors. Take some time to reflect on the following questions:

- What is the first memory you have about money?
- How did your parents or caregivers handle money?
- Do you believe there's a limit to how much money you can earn?
- How do you feel when you receive or spend money?
- What are your thoughts about people who are wealthy?

By answering these questions, you can begin to uncover patterns and limiting beliefs that may be holding you back. For instance, if you often feel guilt when spending money on yourself, it could stem from a deeply ingrained belief that money is scarce and should be hoarded rather than enjoyed.

Shifting from Scarcity to Abundance

Once you've explored your money story and financial mindset, the next step is to shift from a scarcity mindset to an abundance mindset. This shift is not about denying financial challenges but about reframing your perspective to see possibilities rather than limitations.

Understanding Scarcity vs. Abundance in Finances

1. **Scarcity Mindset**
   - Believes there's never enough money.
   - Focuses on what is lacking.
   - Creates fear and anxiety around spending or investing.
   - Views money as a source of stress rather than empowerment.

2. **Abundance Mindset**
   - Believes money is a tool for growth and opportunity.
   - Focuses on what is possible.
   - Encourages gratitude, generosity, and wise financial decisions.
   - Views money as an enabler of dreams and a source of freedom.

Steps to Develop an Abundance Mindset

1. **Acknowledge and Reframe Limiting Beliefs**
   Challenge the negative beliefs uncovered during your reflection. For example, if you believe "I'll never earn enough to live comfortably," reframe it to "I have the skills and creativity to increase my income over time."

2. **Practice Gratitude for Your Current Financial Situation**
   Gratitude shifts your focus from what you lack to what you already have. Begin each day by acknowledging at least one thing you're grateful for regarding your financial life, whether it's the ability to pay bills, a steady income, or even a small amount of savings.

3. **Visualize Financial Abundance**
   Visualization is a powerful tool for shifting your mindset. Picture yourself achieving financial goals—whether it's paying off debt, buying a home, or starting a business. Imagine how abundance would feel and let that vision guide your actions.

4. **Adopt an Opportunity-Oriented Approach**
   Scarcity often makes people risk-averse, but abundance encourages calculated risks. Look for opportunities to grow your wealth, such as learning new skills, pursuing side income, or investing wisely.

5. **Set Financial Goals and Celebrate Progress**
   Clear goals give you direction and purpose. Break them into smaller, achievable steps, and celebrate each milestone. Recognizing progress reinforces the belief that abundance is attainable.

6. **Surround Yourself with an Abundance-Minded Community**

   Spend time with people who inspire and uplift you financially. Their positive energy and attitudes will reinforce your own abundance mindset.

Building a New Money Story

As you shift your mindset, you'll begin to see money as an ally rather than an adversary. Your new money story will reflect a narrative of empowerment, resilience, and possibility. You'll no longer be trapped by the limiting beliefs of scarcity but will instead embrace the freedom and creativity that come with abundance.

Your money story is not static—it evolves as you grow and learn. By exploring your financial mindset and actively reshaping it, you're taking the first steps toward a life of greater financial confidence and abundance.

The journey to rewriting your money story is not always easy, but it is deeply rewarding. As you move forward, remember that every small action you take—whether it's saving a few dollars, learning about investments, or practicing gratitude—brings you closer to financial freedom.

Chapter 2: Everyday Abundance Practices

Simple Actions That Attract Wealth Through Gratitude, Visualization, and Intention

The journey to financial abundance begins with daily practices that align your thoughts, emotions, and actions with prosperity. Abundance isn't just about how much money you have; it's about how you cultivate a mindset of opportunity, gratitude, and trust in your ability to create wealth. This chapter explores simple, actionable steps to attract wealth and establish abundance in your everyday life. By incorporating gratitude, visualization, and intention, you can turn your desires into reality while fostering a deeper sense of fulfillment.

Simple Actions That Attract Wealth

Attracting wealth doesn't always require grand gestures. Small, consistent actions, rooted in intention and awareness, can transform your relationship with money and invite abundance into your life.

1. Create a Wealth-Friendly Environment

The environment you live and work in has a profound impact on your mindset. Decluttering your physical space can create mental clarity and make room for abundance.

- **Declutter Your Wallet and Workspace**: Organize your wallet or purse, keeping it clean and free of unnecessary items. A tidy space promotes clarity and order, signaling to your subconscious that you're ready to receive wealth.
- **Add Symbols of Wealth**: Incorporate symbols or items that represent prosperity, such as a vision board, a lucky charm, or artwork depicting abundance. These serve as daily reminders of your goals.

2. Pay Yourself First

This timeless financial principle is about prioritizing your own savings or investments before spending on other expenses.

- Allocate a percentage of your income to a savings account or investment fund as soon as you receive it.
- Treat this as a non-negotiable habit, just like paying a bill, to build a sense of financial security and abundance over time.

3. Practice Mindful Spending

Mindful spending helps you make deliberate choices with your money, ensuring it aligns with your values and goals.

- **Track Your Expenses**: Keep a daily or weekly record of where your money goes. Awareness of your spending habits empowers you to make adjustments that promote abundance.
- **Spend on What Brings Joy**: Focus on spending money on experiences or items that truly add value to your life, rather than on fleeting indulgences.

4. Give Generously

Generosity is a powerful way to affirm abundance. When you give freely—whether it's your time, money, or skills—you reinforce the belief that there's more than enough to go around.

- Donate a portion of your income to a cause you care about, or offer your expertise to help someone in need.
- Generosity creates a sense of connection and reminds you that wealth is about more than accumulation—it's about making a positive impact.

5. Create Multiple Streams of Income

Financial abundance often comes from diversifying your income.

- Identify your skills and explore ways to monetize them through freelancing, teaching, or creating digital products.
- Investing in side businesses or passive income opportunities, such as rental properties or stock market investments, can also enhance financial stability.

Gratitude: The Foundation of Abundance

Gratitude is one of the most powerful practices for cultivating abundance. When you focus on what you already have, you attract more of what you desire.

1. Start a Gratitude Journal

Keep a journal where you list three to five things you're grateful for each day. Include aspects of your financial life, such as having enough to cover bills, opportunities to earn, or past financial successes.

2. Express Gratitude for Payments

Instead of feeling stressed about paying bills, shift your perspective. View each payment as evidence of your ability to provide for yourself. For example, when paying your electricity bill, express gratitude for the warmth and light your money has provided.

3. Celebrate Small Wins

No success is too small to celebrate. Whether it's saving $10, finding a great deal, or meeting a financial goal, take time to acknowledge your progress. Celebrating small wins fosters positivity and motivation.

Visualization: Seeing Abundance Before It Arrives

Visualization is the practice of mentally picturing your goals as if they've already been achieved. By vividly imagining success, you train your mind to recognize opportunities and take actions that align with your vision.

1. Create a Clear Vision of Financial Abundance

- Picture your ideal financial situation: What does it look like? How does it feel? Where are you living? What does your day-to-day life include?
- Be specific. For instance, instead of saying, "I want to be rich," imagine having $10,000 in savings, a debt-free lifestyle, or earning a six-figure income.

2. Use a Vision Board

- Gather images, quotes, and symbols that represent your financial goals and place them on a board or digital collage.
- Keep this board in a space where you'll see it daily as a reminder of what you're working toward.

3. Visualize Daily

- Spend 5–10 minutes each morning visualizing your goals as if they've already been achieved. Close your eyes and immerse yourself in the details, emotions, and sensations of financial abundance.

Intention: Aligning Your Actions with Your Desires

Intention is the bridge between your thoughts and actions. It's the purposeful decision to align everything you do with your financial goals.

1. Set Daily Intentions

- Begin each day with a clear financial intention, such as "I will make a smart investment today" or "I will save $20 from my grocery budget."
- Write your intention down and reflect on it throughout the day.

2. Be Present in Your Financial Decisions

- Avoid making impulsive financial choices. Pause and ask yourself, "Does this align with my goals?"
- When spending money, do so with awareness and confidence, knowing that each action supports your financial vision.

3. Combine Intention with Affirmations

- Use positive affirmations to reinforce your financial intentions. For example, repeat phrases like:
    - "I am open to receiving wealth in all forms."
    - "I make wise financial decisions every day."
    - "Money flows to me effortlessly and abundantly."

Putting It All Together

Everyday abundance practices—simple actions, gratitude, visualization, and intention—work together to shift your financial reality. These practices create a feedback loop of positivity: gratitude enhances your perspective, visualization keeps you focused on your goals, and intention ensures your actions are purposeful and aligned.

Incorporating these practices into your daily routine doesn't just attract wealth; it transforms the way you view and interact with money. You'll begin to see opportunities where others see obstacles, approach financial challenges with confidence, and create a life of abundance that reflects your highest aspirations.

Chapter 3: Wealth Multiplication Habits

Building Daily Habits for Financial Growth and Time-Tested Principles for Money Management

Wealth is rarely the result of a single windfall or dramatic decision. Instead, it is built and sustained through consistent, deliberate habits that promote financial growth. By cultivating daily practices and adhering to time-tested money management principles, you can create a foundation for long-term wealth. This chapter explores how to develop habits that multiply your wealth and practical strategies that have stood the test of time for effective money management.

Building Daily Habits for Financial Growth

Your daily habits are the small, consistent actions that shape your financial reality. Over time, these habits accumulate, creating significant changes in your wealth. The key to financial growth lies in identifying and implementing habits that align with your goals and values.

1. Automate Your Savings and Investments

Automation ensures that saving and investing become effortless and consistent.

- **Set Up Automatic Transfers**: Arrange for a portion of your income to be transferred automatically to a savings account, retirement fund, or investment portfolio.
- **Use Round-Up Apps**: Apps that round up your purchases to the nearest dollar and save the difference can help you build wealth passively.
- **Pay Yourself First**: Treat your savings and investments as non-negotiable expenses. Automating these contributions ensures you prioritize your financial growth before discretionary spending.

2. Track Your Spending Daily

Awareness is the first step to control. Tracking your spending helps you identify patterns, eliminate waste, and make more informed decisions.

- **Keep a Spending Journal**: At the end of each day, jot down every expense, no matter how small.
- **Use Budgeting Apps**: Digital tools can categorize your spending and provide insights into where your money is going.
- **Set a "Daily Money Check-In"**: Spend five minutes reviewing your financial activity for the day, ensuring it aligns with your goals.

3. Practice the "1% Rule"

Commit to improving your financial habits by just 1% each day.

- **Save 1% More**: Increase your savings rate incrementally. For example, if you save 10% of your income, aim for 11% next month.
- **Invest in Your Knowledge**: Dedicate time to learning about finances daily—read an article, watch a video, or take a short course.
- **Cut Costs by 1%**: Look for small ways to reduce expenses, such as negotiating a lower rate for a subscription or choosing generic brands.

4. Build an Abundance Morning Routine

Starting your day with intention and focus can set the tone for financial success.

- **Gratitude Practice**: Begin by listing three things you're grateful for, especially related to money or opportunities.
- **Review Your Financial Goals**: Spend a few minutes visualizing the life you're building through financial growth.
- **Set a Daily Financial Intention**: Decide on one small action to move closer to your goals, such as making an extra payment toward debt or researching investment options.

5. Foster a Growth-Oriented Network

The people you surround yourself with influence your habits and mindset.

- **Engage with Financially Savvy Individuals**: Join groups or forums where people discuss personal finance, investing, and wealth-building strategies.
- **Seek Mentorship**: Find a mentor who has achieved the level of financial success you aspire to and learn from their experiences.
- **Eliminate Negative Influences**: Distance yourself from individuals who discourage your financial growth or promote unhealthy spending habits.

Time-Tested Principles for Money Management

Effective money management requires discipline and adherence to principles that have proven successful over time. These strategies provide a roadmap for managing, growing, and preserving wealth.

1. Live Below Your Means

This principle is the cornerstone of financial stability and growth.

- **Prioritize Needs Over Wants**: Focus on necessities and limit spending on luxuries until you've achieved financial security.
- **Adopt a Minimalist Approach**: Embrace simplicity by valuing quality over quantity, reducing impulse purchases, and finding contentment in what you already have.

2. Follow the 50/30/20 Rule

This budgeting method divides your income into three categories:

- **50% for Needs**: Rent/mortgage, utilities, groceries, and essential expenses.
- **30% for Wants**: Entertainment, dining out, and non-essentials.
- **20% for Savings and Debt Repayment**: Allocate this portion to building wealth and paying off financial obligations.

Adjust the percentages to suit your financial goals, but ensure that savings and investments are always prioritized.

3. Eliminate Debt Strategically

Debt is one of the biggest obstacles to wealth. Reducing and managing it is crucial for financial growth.

- **Use the Debt Snowball Method**: Pay off the smallest debts first to build momentum, then tackle larger ones.
- **Consider the Debt Avalanche Method**: Prioritize debts with the highest interest rates to minimize long-term costs.

- **Avoid New Debt**: Limit the use of credit cards and focus on paying with cash or savings whenever possible.

4. Invest for the Long Term

Investing is one of the most effective ways to multiply wealth.

- **Start Early**: The power of compounding means the sooner you invest, the more your money grows.
- **Diversify Your Portfolio**: Spread investments across various asset classes, such as stocks, bonds, and real estate, to reduce risk.
- **Be Patient**: Wealth-building takes time. Avoid making impulsive decisions based on short-term market fluctuations.

5. Build and Maintain an Emergency Fund

An emergency fund is a financial safety net that protects you from unexpected expenses.

- **Save 3–6 Months of Living Expenses**: This provides a cushion for job loss, medical emergencies, or other unforeseen events.
- **Keep It Accessible**: Store your emergency fund in a high-yield savings account or a similarly liquid option.
- **Replenish After Use**: If you dip into your emergency fund, prioritize rebuilding it as soon as possible.

6. Protect Your Wealth

Preserving your wealth is as important as building it.

- **Get Adequate Insurance**: Health, life, and property insurance safeguard against significant financial losses.
- **Create an Estate Plan**: Ensure your wealth is distributed according to your wishes by drafting a will or trust.
- **Monitor for Fraud**: Regularly check bank and credit card statements to detect unauthorized transactions.

Habits in Action

Imagine this: You start your day with a gratitude practice, review your financial goals, and set a daily intention to make one small money-smart decision. Throughout the day, you track your expenses, practice mindful spending, and transfer a portion of your income to savings automatically. Over time, these habits compound, leading to measurable financial growth.

Meanwhile, you adhere to proven money management principles, ensuring that your wealth is not only growing but also protected and sustainable. You reduce debt, invest wisely, and maintain a solid emergency fund. Together, these habits and principles form the foundation of a financial strategy that multiplies wealth and creates lasting abundance.

Moving Forward

Building wealth is not about luck or shortcuts—it's about the consistent application of habits and principles that promote financial growth. By incorporating these practices into your daily life, you'll create a system for multiplying your wealth while enjoying greater peace of mind and financial freedom.

Chapter 4: Giving to Receive

How Generosity Unlocks Abundance and the Energy of Reciprocity

At the heart of every abundance mindset lies a profound truth: the act of giving creates a flow of energy that invites abundance into your life. Generosity is not just a moral virtue—it's a practical tool for growth and a catalyst for prosperity. When you give with intention and an open heart, you tap into the universal law of reciprocity, where the energy you put out into the world returns to you multiplied. This chapter explores the transformative power of generosity, how it unlocks abundance, and the principles of reciprocity that underpin this flow.

How Generosity Unlocks Abundance

The act of giving transcends monetary value. Whether you give your time, skills, resources, or attention, generosity creates a ripple effect that touches lives, fosters connections, and amplifies abundance for everyone involved.

1. Shifting from Lack to Overflow

Generosity helps reframe your relationship with abundance.

- **The Scarcity Trap**: When operating from a scarcity mindset, you may feel compelled to hoard resources out of fear that there isn't enough to go around. This creates a mental and emotional block, preventing you from recognizing opportunities for growth.
- **The Overflow Mentality**: Giving, even in small ways, shifts your focus from lack to overflow. By sharing what you have, you affirm to yourself and the universe that there is enough, and more will always come your way.

Example: If you tip generously at a coffee shop, you're reinforcing a belief in your ability to provide for others and yourself. This act of kindness generates goodwill and often inspires others to do the same.

2. Building Trust and Relationships

Generosity is a cornerstone of meaningful connections.

- **Fostering Trust**: When you give without expecting anything in return, you build trust and goodwill in your relationships. This often leads to opportunities and support that wouldn't have arisen otherwise.
- **Strengthening Networks**: Whether in personal or professional circles, people are drawn to those who uplift and contribute selflessly. A reputation for generosity can open doors to partnerships, collaborations, and unexpected blessings.

3. Creating a Ripple Effect of Positivity

Acts of generosity inspire others to pay it forward.

- **Social Contagion of Kindness**: Studies show that when people witness generosity, they're more likely to emulate it. Your actions can create a chain reaction of giving that impacts countless lives.
- **Community Growth**: Generosity strengthens communities, fostering an environment of mutual support where everyone has the opportunity to thrive.

4. Inviting Opportunity Through Contribution

The more you contribute to the world, the more opportunities find their way to you.

- **The Principle of Value Exchange**: When you provide value—whether through teaching, mentoring, or offering resources—you position yourself as an indispensable part of a larger ecosystem.

- **Reputation as a Giver**: Generosity enhances your personal brand, making others more inclined to collaborate with, support, or recommend you.

The Energy of Reciprocity

Reciprocity is the universal law that what you give comes back to you, often in unexpected and multiplied ways. This concept is not just philosophical—it's supported by principles of human psychology, economics, and even spirituality.

1. Understanding the Flow of Energy

Every act of giving creates a flow of energy that connects you to others.

- **Money as Energy**: Money is a medium of exchange, representing energy in motion. When you circulate money through giving, you keep the flow active and invite more energy (wealth) into your life.
- **Emotional Resonance**: Giving generates positive emotions for both the giver and the receiver, creating a shared experience of abundance that enhances well-being.

2. The Boomerang Effect

What you give, you receive in return, often in magnified forms.

- **The Multiplication Principle**: While the return may not be immediate or from the same source, acts of generosity often lead to unexpected blessings. For instance, donating to a cause may lead to meeting someone who offers a career opportunity or sharing your expertise may result in a recommendation for a lucrative project.
- **Creating Space for Receiving**: When you give, you signal that you're open to receiving. The space you create by giving freely allows new opportunities and resources to flow in.

3. Aligning Intentions with Giving

Giving with pure intention amplifies its impact.

- **Avoid Transactional Giving**: Generosity rooted in the expectation of immediate returns can block the flow of reciprocity. True abundance stems from giving without strings attached.
- **Cultivate Joy in Giving**: When you give from a place of joy and fulfillment, the energy you emit is positive and magnetic, drawing abundance to you naturally.

4. Balancing Giving and Receiving

While generosity is vital, it's equally important to remain open to receiving.

- **Avoid Over-Giving**: Giving beyond your means or neglecting your own needs can lead to burnout. Balance generosity with self-care and financial prudence.
- **Embrace Receiving**: Many people struggle with accepting help or gifts, feeling unworthy or indebted. Remember, receiving is part of the energy exchange and allows others to experience the joy of giving.

Practical Ways to Practice Generosity

Generosity doesn't have to involve large financial contributions. It's about sharing what you can in ways that are meaningful to you and beneficial to others.

1. Share Your Time

- Volunteer for a cause you believe in.
- Offer to mentor or support someone in your network.
- Spend quality time with friends or family members who need encouragement.

2. Use Your Skills to Give Back

- Provide pro-bono services for a nonprofit or a friend in need.
- Teach a class or workshop on a topic you're passionate about.
- Create resources, such as free guides or tools, to help others succeed.

3. Financial Contributions

- Donate to charities or causes that resonate with you.
- Support local businesses or artists by purchasing their products.
- Set aside a small portion of your income for acts of kindness, such as buying a meal for someone in need.

4. Random Acts of Kindness

- Pay for the coffee of the person behind you in line.
- Write a heartfelt note to someone who has impacted your life.
- Surprise a friend with a thoughtful gift or gesture.

Cultivating a Generous Spirit

Generosity is not just about external actions; it's a way of being. Cultivating a generous spirit means approaching life with an open heart and a willingness to contribute wherever you can.

- **Practice Gratitude Daily**: Gratitude fosters a mindset of abundance, making it easier to give.
- **Be Present in Your Giving**: Engage fully in acts of generosity, focusing on the connection and impact rather than the outcome.
- **Celebrate the Wins of Others**: Genuinely rejoice in the successes of those around you, knowing that their abundance does not diminish your own.

Moving Forward

Generosity and reciprocity form the foundation of a life filled with abundance. By giving freely and embracing the energy of exchange, you create a flow that invites prosperity and strengthens your connections to others. Each act of kindness, no matter how small, contributes to a larger cycle of growth and opportunity.

Chapter 5: Living Abundantly

Embodying Wealth in All Areas of Life and Balancing Success with Fulfillment

True abundance is not just about financial wealth; it encompasses all areas of life—relationships, health, purpose, and personal growth. Living abundantly means embodying a mindset of prosperity and fulfillment, where success is measured not only by material gains but by the richness of your experiences, connections, and contributions. In this chapter, we'll explore how to live abundantly by aligning your actions, mindset, and goals with holistic wealth while maintaining a balance between success and fulfillment.

Embodying Wealth in All Areas of Life

Living abundantly requires expanding your definition of wealth beyond money. When you embody abundance in every area of life, you create a harmonious existence that supports your well-being and amplifies your prosperity.

1. Financial Abundance: Building Prosperity with Purpose

Financial abundance serves as a foundation, enabling freedom and opportunities.

- **Create a Vision of Financial Freedom**: Define what financial abundance looks like for you. Is it debt-free living? The ability to travel? Retiring early? Use this vision to guide your decisions.
- **Use Money as a Tool**: View money as a resource to invest in your goals, dreams, and personal development rather than as an end in itself.
- **Celebrate Financial Milestones**: Acknowledge and celebrate small financial wins, such as saving your first $1,000, paying off a loan, or reaching an investment goal.

2. Emotional Abundance: Cultivating Inner Wealth

Emotional abundance stems from a mindset of gratitude, resilience, and self-awareness.

- **Practice Daily Gratitude**: Reflect on what you appreciate in your life, from small joys to significant accomplishments. Gratitude shifts your focus from lack to abundance.
- **Develop Emotional Resilience**: Challenges are inevitable, but a resilient mindset allows you to navigate them with grace and optimism.
- **Invest in Self-Care**: Prioritize activities that nurture your emotional well-being, such as meditation, journaling, or spending time in nature.

3. Relationship Abundance: Building Meaningful Connections

Abundant living includes thriving relationships built on trust, love, and mutual respect.

- **Prioritize Quality Over Quantity**: Focus on deepening relationships with those who uplift and inspire you.
- **Give Without Expectation**: Acts of kindness and generosity strengthen connections and create a positive ripple effect.
- **Communicate Openly**: Honest, empathetic communication fosters trust and strengthens bonds.

4. Physical Abundance: Embracing Health and Vitality

Physical abundance involves taking care of your body so that it supports your ability to live fully and energetically.

- **Nurture Your Body**: Eat nourishing foods, stay active, and prioritize rest to maintain your physical health.
- **Listen to Your Body's Needs**: Recognize the signals your body sends and respond with care and attention.
- **Celebrate Your Strengths**: Appreciate the unique abilities and resilience of your body rather than focusing on perceived flaws.

5. Spiritual Abundance: Connecting to Something Greater

Spiritual abundance is about finding meaning and purpose in your life.

- **Define Your Purpose**: Reflect on what gives your life meaning, whether it's helping others, pursuing creative passions, or exploring your spirituality.
- **Stay Present**: Practice mindfulness to connect with the present moment and cultivate a sense of peace.
- **Seek Growth**: Continuously explore ways to deepen your understanding of yourself and the world around you.

Balancing Success with Fulfillment

While success is often associated with achievement and external recognition, fulfillment comes from aligning your goals with your values and living authentically. Striking a balance between the two ensures that your journey toward abundance is both rewarding and sustainable.

1. Redefine Success on Your Terms

Success should reflect your unique aspirations and values, not societal expectations.

- **Clarify Your Core Values**: Identify what matters most to you—family, creativity, freedom, or making a difference—and align your goals with these values.
- **Measure Success Holistically**: Consider how your achievements contribute to your overall well-being, relationships, and happiness, not just your financial status.

2. Avoid the Burnout Trap

Pursuing success at the expense of your health and happiness can lead to burnout.

- **Set Boundaries**: Protect your time and energy by saying no to commitments that don't align with your goals.
- **Schedule Downtime**: Prioritize rest and relaxation as essential components of productivity and creativity.
- **Focus on Progress, Not Perfection**: Striving for perfection can be exhausting. Celebrate progress and learn from setbacks without self-judgment.

3. Cultivate Joy in the Present Moment

Fulfillment comes from appreciating where you are while striving for where you want to be.

- **Practice Mindfulness**: Stay present and fully engaged in your daily activities, whether working, spending time with loved ones, or pursuing hobbies.
- **Celebrate Small Wins**: Acknowledge and savor everyday victories, from completing a task to sharing a meaningful conversation.
- **Create Rituals of Joy**: Incorporate moments of joy into your routine, such as a morning coffee ritual, an evening walk, or a gratitude practice.

4. Give Back as a Path to Fulfillment

Contributing to others enhances your sense of purpose and connection.

- **Volunteer Your Time**: Offer your skills or resources to support causes that resonate with you.
- **Mentor or Teach**: Share your knowledge and experiences to uplift others.
- **Celebrate Others' Successes**: Supporting and celebrating others' achievements creates a community of abundance and mutual growth.

Living Abundantly in Action

Imagine a life where financial security enables you to travel, pursue passions, and support loved ones; where your emotional and physical health allow you to experience each day with energy and joy; and where your relationships and sense of purpose provide deep fulfillment. This is the essence of living abundantly.

To embody this lifestyle:

- **Commit to Daily Practices**: Incorporate habits that support your financial, emotional, physical, and spiritual well-being.
- **Balance Action and Reflection**: Pursue your goals with intention while regularly reflecting on whether they align with your values.
- **Celebrate and Share Abundance**: Recognize the abundance in your life and share it with others to amplify its impact.

Moving Forward

Living abundantly is not a destination but an ongoing journey. By embodying wealth in all areas of life and balancing success with fulfillment, you create a life rich in experiences, connections, and opportunities. In the next chapter, we'll explore strategies for overcoming obstacles that may hinder your abundance journey and practical tools to stay resilient and focused.

Appendix A: Wealth Trackers and Affirmations

To support your journey toward abundance, practical tools and positive affirmations can play a significant role in maintaining focus and cultivating a prosperous mindset. This appendix provides detailed instructions for creating wealth trackers to monitor your progress, alongside affirmations to reinforce a mindset of abundance and growth.

Wealth Trackers: Tools for Monitoring Progress

Tracking your financial progress is essential for accountability and motivation. Wealth trackers help you visualize where you stand, identify areas for improvement, and celebrate milestones.

1. Monthly Income and Expense Tracker

This tracker helps you monitor your cash flow by recording income and expenses.

How to Use:

1. **Create Categories**: Divide income into sources (e.g., salary, side hustles, investments) and expenses into categories (e.g., housing, utilities, food, entertainment, savings).
2. **Set Goals**: Assign a monthly goal for savings or discretionary spending to keep you on track.
3. **Record Daily Transactions**: Log every transaction to gain a clear picture of your financial behavior.
4. **Review Monthly**: At the end of the month, analyze whether you met your goals, identify overspending, and adjust accordingly.

Template:

Date	Income Source	Amount ($)	Expense Category	Amount ($)	Notes
Jan 1	Salary	3000	Rent	1200	Paid on time
Jan 3	Freelance Project	500	Groceries	300	Budgeted correctly

2. Debt Reduction Tracker

Paying off debt is a significant step toward financial freedom. This tracker helps you monitor your progress in reducing debt.

How to Use:

1. **List Debts**: Include all debts, such as credit cards, student loans, or car payments, with interest rates and minimum payments.
2. **Choose a Strategy**: Use the debt snowball method (start with the smallest debt) or the debt avalanche method (focus on highest interest rate first).
3. **Track Payments**: Log each payment, reducing the debt balance accordingly.
4. **Celebrate Milestones**: Reward yourself for every debt cleared or major milestone reached.

Template:

Debt Name	Total Amount ($)	Interest Rate (%)	Minimum Payment ($)	Monthly Payment ($)	Remaining Balance ($)
Credit Card A	5000	18.5	150	200	4800
Student Loan B	20000	6.5	300	400	19600

3. Savings Goal Tracker

Tracking savings builds momentum and helps you visualize progress toward financial goals.

How to Use:

1. **Define Your Goal**: Determine a target amount and deadline (e.g., $5,000 for a vacation in 12 months).
2. **Break It Down**: Divide the goal into monthly or weekly savings amounts.
3. **Track Deposits**: Record every deposit made toward the goal.
4. **Visualize Progress**: Use charts, graphs, or thermometers to illustrate how close you are to your goal.

Template:

Goal	Target Amount ($)	Dead-line	Monthly Savings Target ($)	Total Saved ($)	Progress (%)
Emergency Fund	10000	Dec 2025	500	3500	35%

4. Investment Portfolio Tracker

Monitor the growth and diversification of your investments.

How to Use:

1. **List Investments**: Include stocks, bonds, mutual funds, real estate, or any other investments.
2. **Track Performance**: Record changes in value, dividends, or returns.
3. **Evaluate Diversification**: Ensure your portfolio is balanced across various asset classes.
4. **Adjust Regularly**: Use insights from the tracker to make informed investment decisions.

Template:

Investment Type	Initial Value ($)	Current Value ($)	Change ($)	ROI (%)	Notes
Stock A	1000	1200	+200	20%	High growth potential
Real Estate	50000	55000	+5000	10%	Long-term investment

Affirmations: Reprogramming Your Mindset

Affirmations are powerful tools for shifting beliefs, focusing on abundance, and reinforcing positive financial behaviors. By repeating these affirmations regularly, you create neural pathways that support your abundance mindset.

1. Daily Abundance Affirmations

These affirmations help you cultivate a mindset of wealth and possibility.

- "I am a magnet for wealth and abundance."
- "Money flows to me effortlessly and abundantly."
- "I am open to receiving all forms of prosperity."
- "I am financially free and secure."
- "I attract opportunities to grow my wealth."

2. Gratitude-Based Affirmations

Gratitude reinforces your awareness of existing abundance.

- "I am grateful for the financial blessings I have now."
- "Every day, I find new reasons to be thankful for my wealth."
- "I appreciate all the ways money supports my life."
- "My gratitude multiplies my abundance."
- "I am thankful for the opportunities I have to create wealth."

3. Empowerment Affirmations

These affirmations build confidence in your ability to manage and grow wealth.

- "I make wise financial decisions every day."
- "I am capable of achieving all my financial goals."
- "I have the power to create the financial future I desire."
- "I am in control of my money, and my money works for me."
- "I release all fears and doubts about wealth."

4. Affirmations for Giving and Receiving

These affirmations align your actions with the energy of reciprocity.

- "The more I give, the more I receive in return."
- "I share my wealth with joy and generosity."
- "I am open to receiving financial abundance from unexpected sources."
- "I trust the universe to provide for all my needs."
- "My giving creates a ripple effect of prosperity for others and myself."

How to Use Affirmations Effectively

1. **Repeat Daily**: Say your affirmations aloud or write them in a journal every morning and evening.
2. **Visualize While Repeating**: Imagine yourself living the reality described in your affirmations.
3. **Feel the Emotions**: Connect with the joy, gratitude, and confidence that abundance brings.
4. **Place Reminders**: Write affirmations on sticky notes and place them in visible locations, such as your mirror, desk, or phone background.
5. **Combine with Action**: Pair affirmations with deliberate actions that align with your financial goals.

By using wealth trackers to monitor your progress and affirmations to reinforce your abundance mindset, you'll create a powerful system for achieving and sustaining financial growth. These tools not only keep you accountable but also keep you motivated and inspired to live abundantly in all areas of life.

<u>Message from the Author:</u>

I hope you enjoyed this book, I love astrology and knew there was not a book such as this out on the shelf. I love metaphysical items as well. Please check out my other books:

-Life of Government Benefits

-My life of Hell

-My life with Hydrocephalus

-Red Sky

-World Domination:Woman's rule

-World Domination:Woman's Rule 2: The War

-Life and Banishment of Apophis: book 1

-The Kidney Friendly Diet

-The Ultimate Hemp Cookbook

-Creating a Dispensary(legally)

-Cleanliness throughout life: the importance of showering from childhood to adulthood.

-Strong Roots: The Risks of Overcoddling children

-Hemp Horoscopes: Cosmic Insights and Earthly Healing

- Celestial Hemp Navigating the Zodiac: Through the Green Cosmos

-Astrological Hemp: Aligning The Stars with Earth's Ancient Herb

-The Astrological Guide to Hemp: Stars, Signs, and Sacred Leaves

-Green Growth: Innovative Marketing Strategies for your Hemp Products and Dispensary

-Cosmic Cannabis

-Astrological Munchies

-Henry The Hemp

-Zodiacal Roots: The Astrological Soul Of Hemp

- **Green Constellations: Intersection of Hemp and Zodiac**

-Hemp in The Houses: An astrological Adventure Through The Cannabis Galaxy

-Galactic Ganja Guide

Heavenly Hemp

Zodiac Leaves

Doctor Who Astrology

Cannastrology

Stellar Satvias and Cosmic Indicas

Celestial Cannabis: A Zodiac Journey

AstroHerbology: The Sky and The Soil: Volume 1

AstroHerbology:Celestial Cannabis:Volume 2

Cosmic Cannabis Cultivation

The Starry Guide to Herbal Harmony: Volume 1

The Starry Guide to Herbal Harmony: Cannabis Universe: Volume 2

Yugioh Astrology: Astrological Guide to Deck, Duels and more

Nightmare Mansion: Echoes of The Abyss

Nightmare Mansion 2: Legacy of Shadows

Nightmare Mansion 3: Shadows of the Forgotten

Nightmare Mansion 4: Echoes of the Damned

The Life and Banishment of Apophis: Book 2

Nightmare Mansion: Halls of Despair

Healing with Herb: Cannabis and Hydrocephalus

Planetary Pot: Aligning with Astrological Herbs: Volume 1

Fast Track to Freedom: 30 Days to Financial Independence Using AI, Assets, and Agile Hustles

Cosmic Hemp Pathways

How to Become Financially Free in 30 Days: 10,000 Paths to Prosperity

Zodiacal Herbage: Astrological Insights: Volume 1

Nightmare Mansion: Whispers in the Walls

The Daleks Invade Atlantis

Henry the hemp and Hydrocephalus

10X The Kidney Friendly Diet

Cannabis Universe: Adult coloring book

Hemp Astrology: The Healing Power of the Stars

Zodiacal Herbage: Astrological Insights: Cannabis Universe: Volume 2

<u>Planetary Pot: Aligning with Astrological Herbs: Cannabis Universes: Volume 2</u>

Doctor Who Meets the Replicators and SG-1: The Ultimate Battle for Survival

Nightmare Mansion: Curse of the Blood Moon

<u>The Celestial Stoner: A Guide to the Zodiac</u>

Cosmic Pleasures: Sex Toy Astrology for Every Sign

Hydrocephalus Astrology: Navigating the Stars and Healing Waters

Lapis and the Mischievous Chocolate Bar

Celestial Positions: Sexual Astrology for Every Sign

Apophis's Shadow Work Journal: **:** A Journey of Self-Discovery and Healing

Kinky Cosmos: Sexual Kink Astrology for Every Sign

Digital Cosmos: The Astrological Digimon Compendium

Stellar Seeds: The Cosmic Guide to Growing with Astrology

Apophis's Daily Gratitude Journal

Cat Astrology: Feline Mysteries of the Cosmos

The Cosmic Kama Sutra: An Astrological Guide to Sexual Positions

Unleash Your Potential: A Guided Journal Powered by AI Insights

Whispers of the Enchanted Grove

Cosmic Pleasures: An Astrological Guide to Sexual Kinks

369, 12 Manifestation Journal

Whisper of the nocturne journal(blank journal for writing or draw-ing)

The Boogey Book

Locked In Reflection: A Chastity Journey Through Locktober

Generating Wealth Quickly:

How to Generate $100,000 in 24 Hours

Star Magic: Harness the Power of the Universe

The Flatulence Chronicles: A Fart Journal for Self-Discovery

The Doctor and The Death Moth

Seize the Day: A Personal Seizure Tracking Journal

The Ultimate Boogeyman Safari: A Journey into the Boogie World and Beyond

Whispers of Samhain: 1,000 Spells of Love, Luck, and Lunar Magic: Samhain Spell Book

Apophis's guides:

Witch's Spellbook Crafting Guide for Halloween

<u>Frost & Flame: The Enchanted Yule Grimoire of 1000 Winter Spells</u>

<u>The Ultimate Boogey Goo Guide & Spooky Activities for Halloween Fun</u>

Harmony of the Scales: A Libra's Spellcraft for Balance and Beauty

The Enchanted Advent: 36 Days of Christmas Wonders

Nightmare Mansion: The Labyrinth of Screams

Harvest of Enchantment: 1,000 Spells of Gratitude, Love, and Fortune for Thanksgiving

The Boogey Chronicles: A Journal of Nightly Encounters and Shadowy Secrets

The 12 Days of Financial Freedom: A Step-by-Step Christmas Countdown to Transform Your Finances

Sigil of the Eternal Spiral Blank Journal

A Christmas Feast: Timeless Recipes for Every Meal

Holiday Stress-Free Solutions: A Survival Guide to Thriving During the Festive Season

Yu-Gi-Oh! Holiday Gifting Mastery: The Ultimate Guide for Fans and Newcomers Alike

Holiday Harmony: A Hydrocephalus Survival Guide for the Festive Season

Celestial Craft: The Witch's Almanac for 2025 – A Cosmic Guide to Manifestations, Moons, and Mystical Events

Doctor Who: The Toymaker's Winter Wonderland

Tulsa King Unveiled: A Thrilling Guide to Stallone's Mafia Masterpiece

Pendulum Craft: A Complete Guide to Crafting and Using Personalized Divination Tools

Nightmare Mansion: Santa's Eternal Eve

Starlight Noel: A Cosmic Journey through Christmas Mysteries

The Dark Architect: Unlocking the Blueprint of Existence

Surviving the Embrace: The Ultimate Guide to Encounters with The Hugging Molly

The Enchanted Codex: Secrets of the Craft for Witches, Wiccans, and Pagans

Harvest of Gratitude: A Complete Thanksgiving Guide

Yuletide Essentials: A Complete Guide to an Authentic and Magical Christmas

Celestial Smokes: A Cosmic Guide to Cigars and Astrology

Living in Balance: A Comprehensive Survival Guide to Thriving with Diabetes Insipidus

Cosmic Symbiosis: The Venom Zodiac Chronicles

The Cursed Paw of Ambition

Cosmic Symbiosis: The Astrological Venom Journal

Celestial Wonders Unfold: A Stargazer's Guide to the Cosmos (2024-2029)

The Ultimate Black Friday Prepper's Guide: Mastering Shopping Strategies and Savings

Cosmic Sales: The Astrological Guide to Black Friday Shopping

Legends of the Corn Mother and Other Harvest Myths

Whispers of the Harvest: The Corn Mother's Journal

The Evergreen Spellbook

The Doctor Meets the Boogeyman

The White Witch of Rose Hall's SpellBook

The Gingerbread Golem's Shadow: A Study in Sweet Darkness

The Gingerbread Golem Codex: An Academic Exploration of Sweet Myths

The Gingerbread Golem Grimoire: Sweet Magicks and Spells for the Festive Witch

The Curse of the Gingerbread Golem

10-minute Christmas Crafts for kids

<u>Christmas Crisis Solutions: The Ultimate Last-Minute Survival Guide</u>

Gingerbread Golem Recipes: Holiday Treats with a Magical Twist

The Infinite Key: Unlocking Mystical Secrets of the Ages

Enchanted Yule: A Wiccan and Pagan Guide to a Magical and Memorable Season

Dinosaurs of Power: Unlocking Ancient Magick

Astro-Dinos: The Cosmic Guide to Prehistoric Wisdom

Gallifrey's Yule Logs: A Festive Doctor Who Cookbook

The Dino Grimoire: Secrets of Prehistoric Magick

The Gift They Never Knew They Needed

The Gingerbread Golem's Culinary Alchemy: Enchanting Recipes for a Sweetly Dark Feast

A Time Lord Christmas: Holiday Adventures with the Doctor

Krampusproofing Your Home: Defensive Strategies for Yule

Silent Frights: A Collection of Christmas Creepypastas to Chill Your Bones

Santa Raptor's Jolly Carnage: A Dino-Claus Christmas Tale

Prehistoric Palettes: A Dino Wicca Coloring Journey

The Christmas Wishkeeper Chronicles

The Starlight Sleigh: A Holiday Journey
Elf Secrets: The True Magic of the North Pole
Candy Cane Conjurations
Cooking with Kids: Recipes Under 20 Minutes
Doctor Who: The TARDIS Confiscation
The Anxiety First Aid Kit: Quick Tools to Calm Your Mind
Frosty Whispers: A Winter's Tale
The Infinite Key: Unlocking the Secrets to Prosperity, Resilience, and Purpose
The Grasping Void: Why You'll Regret This Purchase
Astrology for Busy Bees: Star Signs Simplified
The Instant Focus Formula: Cut Through the Noise
The Secret Language of Colors: Unlocking the Emotional Codes
Sacred Fossil Chronicles: Blank Journal
The Christmas Cottage Miracle
Feeding Frenzy: Graboid-Inspired Recipes
Manifest in Minutes: The Quick Law of Attraction Guide
The Symbiote Chronicles: Doctor Who's Venomous Journey
Think Tiny, Grow Big: The Minimalist Mindset
The Energy Key: Unlocking Limitless Motivation
New Year, New Magic: Manifesting Your Best Year Yet
Unstoppable You: Mastering Confidence in Minutes
Infinite Energy: The Secret to Never Feeling Drained
Lightning Focus: Mastering the Art of Productivity in a Distracted World
Saturnalia Manifestation Magick: A Guide to Unlocking Abundance During the Solstice
Graboids and Garland: The Ultimate Tremors-Themed Christmas Guide
12 Nights of Holiday Magic
The Power of Pause: 60-Second Mindfulness Practices
The Quick Reset: How to Reclaim Your Life After Burnout
The Shadow Eater: A Tale of Despair and Survival

The Micro-Mastery Method: Transform Your Skills in Just Minutes a Day

Reclaiming Time: How to Live More by Doing Less

Chronovore: The Eternal Nexus

The Mind Reset: Unlocking Your Inner Peace in a Chaotic World

Confidence Code: Building Unshakable Self-Belief

Baby the Vampire Terrier

Baby the Vampire Terrier's Christmas Adventure

Celestial Streams: The Content Creator's Astrology Manual

If you want solar for your home go here: https://www.harborsolar.live/apophisenterprises/

Get Some Tarot cards: https://www.makeplayingcards.com/sell/apophis-occult-shop

<u>**Get some shirts: https://www.bonfire.com/store/apophis-shirt-emporium/**</u>

__Instagrams:__
@apophis_enterprises,
@apophisbookemporium,
@apophisscardshop
Twitter: @apophisenterpr1
Tiktok:@apophisenterprise
Youtube: @sg1fan23477, @FiresideRetreatKingdom
Hive: @sg1fan23477
CheeLee: @SG1fan23477
Podcast: Apophis Chat Zone: https://open.spotify.com/show/5zXbrCLEV2xzCp8ybrfHsk?si=fb4d4fdbdce44dec

Newsletter: https://apophiss-newsletter-27c897.beehiiv.com/

If you want to support me or see posts of other projects that I have come over to: **<u>buymeacoffee.com/mpetchinskg</u>**
I post there daily several times a day

Get your Dinowicca or Christmas themed digital products, especially Santa Raptor songs and other musics. Here: **https://sg1fan23477.gumroad.com**

Apophis Yuletide Digital has not only digital Christmas items, but it will have all things with Dinowicca as well as other Digital products.

www.ingramcontent.com/pod-product-compliance
Lightning Source LLC
Chambersburg PA
CBHW060914130726
48001CB00006B/2239